Magical Mathematics

Five Astonishing Stories of People Who Did Miracles with Numbers

Nury Vittachi

Illustrations by Step Cheung

Contents

THE GIRL, THE PEARL AND THE NOT-SO-SAD STORY

ONE BRIGHT DAY MORE than 900 years ago, a girl and her father sat in the shade of a tree with a pen and paper. They were playing thinking games.

Her nickname was Lilavati, which meant little miss playful.

His name was Bhaskara and he was a professional wise man, a heaven-watching advisor to the rulers.

Their favorite game was mathematics magic: they sat for hours experimenting with numbers, discovering astonishing hidden patterns and surprising answers. Playing this sort of game, Lilavati realized, was fun but it was also an amazing exercise for the brain.

M
$\sqrt{a}=|a|$
α
STEP C

Every sunset, after Lilavati went to sleep, Bhaskara went to work, for stargazing was one of his most important jobs.

From the dawn of time, people have looked to the heavens when thinking about big ideas. Although these days we make a clear difference between astronomers and astrologers, in the past, these ideas were all mixed together. There was no such word as "scientist" until 1832. Instead, for most of recorded history, there were people called Natural Philosophers, who looked at the world around them and tried to understand it.

One day, Bhaskara's stargazer colleagues came to him with some bad news. They said his daughter's star charts predicted that she would not get married or have children.

What could the stargazer do? He knew it was possible for a person to live a happy life without a spouse or children — but he had always felt that Lilavati was destined to be remembered. But who would remember her if she had no offspring?

That night he looked up at stars with his daughter in mind, and considered all the forms of knowledge he could find, from natural philosophy to beliefs about birthdays. Ancient ideas about "auspicious moments" suggested that there was one chance for her to change her destiny.

He got the feeling that if Lilavati chose by herself to get married at one particular time, she might avoid the bad fortune of not having a family. To be childless was considered a sad state of affairs for a woman at that time and in that place: India in the 1100s.

So Bhaskara set to work. He constructed a machine in which water would flow slowly from one part to another, working as a type of clock, to tell the girl when to get married.

He would step away from the house, but the water clock would tell her the right moment.

"Don't go near it," Bhaskara told Lilavati. "Just wait for a signal."

Then he left her alone.

Sitting in her wedding dress, Lilavati waited.

And waited.

And waited.

Then she tiptoed over and peered at the machine. A pearl from her headdress fell into the water — and stopped the machine working.

But Lilavati did not notice.

The auspicious moment passed. And the signal was not given.

Some historians say she missed the right time and decided not to marry. Others say she did get married but at the wrong hour, and her husband died within days, leaving her a young, childless widow.

Whichever it was, we do know that she never became a wife and mother.

Instead, she and her beloved father found themselves together again, both feeling really sad.

But then she had an idea. She got out a piece of paper and a pen and they started playing mathematics games again.

Their smiles returned.

And then Bhaskara decided to capture their games on paper.

A book was published in AD 1150. It was a mathematics textbook, but it was not called "Mathematics Textbook" and it was not filled with exercises.

No. It was called "Lilavati" and was filled with conversations about numbers. It said things like: "Fawn-eyed child Lilavati, what is 135 multiplied by 12, beautiful one?"

The book became one of the top mathematics books in the world. It was used for centuries and taught countless numbers of children the joy of numbers.

Lilavati's friends, who got married and had children in the normal way, have all been forgotten. But nine centuries later, the girl whose love of numbers inspired numerous generations is still remembered.

THE BOY WITH NO BIRTHDAY

ONCE UPON A TIME, there was a boy with no birthday. Carl Gauss had been born on a particular day, just like the rest of us, but no one knew when that was.

His mother was very poor and illiterate, which meant that she could not read or write, so she hadn't written it down.

"It was a Wednesday," she would say. And she would mention a particular church ritual. "And it was eight days before the Feast of Ascension."

His father was poor, too, working outdoors as a gardener and bricklayer in Germany.

But his mother wanted her son to be successful, so she encouraged him to learn writing and mathematics.

STEP C

One day, when Carl was three years old, he saw his father working on a payroll calculation.

"You made a mistake," the boy said, pointing it out. "And I can tell you what the right answer should be."

His father was stunned: his sums were being corrected by a child who was little more than a toddler.

When he was seven, Carl was sent to school. One day, his teacher set his students a challenge: add up all the numbers between 1 and 100 and write down the answer.

Everyone started doing the sums.

But not Carl.

Was it too hard for him?

No, quite the opposite. He told his teacher: "I don't need to add them up. It would obviously be 50 pairs of numbers each totaling 101, so that would be 5,050, right?"

He was right.

The school and his parents realized that they had a genuine genius on their hands. Carl Friedrich Gauss quickly became recognized as one of the greatest mathematicians in history, even while he was just a teenager. Here are some examples of his influence.

1) When Carl Gauss was 19, he managed to solve a math puzzle that had baffled the ancient Greek thinkers, whose wisdom was legendary.

2) He used math to find a lost planet. An astronomer named Giuseppe Piazzi discovered a small planet which he called Ceres. But it seemed to move oddly, and one day it totally disappeared.

Carl asked to look at the data that Piazzi had written down about where and when he had seen the planet Ceres.

The young man then did some math and worked out exactly when and where Ceres would reappear in the night sky — and he turned out to be exactly right.

3) Even today, people use his mathematics to help them. When the technology experts who made the famous software program Adobe Photoshop wanted a way to teach computers to use mathematics to make perfectly soft, fuzzy colors — randomized, but with no blotchy bits — they used Gauss's math to produce a popular photo-editing option called Gaussian Blur.

But best of all, Carl used mathematics to solve the puzzle of his own birthday. By using the clues his mother had given him about the day of the week and the church ritual, he calculated that he was born on Wednesday, April 30, 1777.

At last he knew when to celebrate. Happy birthday, Carl!

THE MATH GIRL WHO STUNNED THE WORLD

ELIZABETH AND MILLICENT GARRETT were two adult sisters who campaigned for women's rights.

This was in the late 1800s. Men would sometimes grudgingly allow women to play small roles in society "as long as they didn't get in the way".

But the sisters felt this was not good enough. They felt women were as clever as men, and could even be smarter: a claim that made their male friends laugh.

Yet the sisters' own lives showed the truth of their claims. Elizabeth became the first female registered doctor and surgeon in the UK. Millicent became a famous campaigner in the fight to give women the right to vote.

These achievements focused on women being treated fairly. But their male critics pointed out that they didn't actually prove that women could be smarter than men.

Meanwhile, the two sisters were happy to note that Millicent's teenage daughter Philippa was clearly super-smart, like the other female members of the family.

The high-achieving Garretts helped set up a college in Cambridge. When Philippa was in her late teens, she was allowed to listen to lectures, although only men were allowed to graduate.

Cambridge offered a famous test called the Mathematical Tripos, said to be the hardest undergraduate exam in the world.

Only a small number of men every year entered it. The men who got first class passes were given the title "wrangler" (which means someone who can handle a really tough problem). Some of the world's top scientists and thinkers had started their careers by becoming wranglers at Cambridge.

Every year, the professor who announced the results would take off his hat when he read the top scorer's name, because it was so difficult to win that spot. That man would be given the title senior wrangler, and people assumed that he would become rich and powerful. (The youngest man ever to win the title of senior wrangler went on to become Prime Minister of Great Britain at the age of 24!)

Women were allowed to take the test, just for fun, but of course could not be on the list of wranglers — those titles were for men only.

When Philippa took the test in 1890, she did her very best, wanting to at least get the same score as some of the young men on the list. It would be brilliant if she got the same score as one of the boys in the top ten.

The list of men who had passed the test was read out, and when a certain young male was named, the chief professor removed his hat. A new senior wrangler had been named!

There was loud applause.

But there was a surprise to come. He then read out the list

of women who had passed the test that year.

And he announced that Philippa's result was "above the senior wrangler".

Everyone was stunned. She'd beaten ALL the men.

Over the next few days, Philippa's name was in newspapers around the world.

"Once again has woman demonstrated her superiority in the face of an incredulous and somewhat unsympathetic world," the Daily Telegraph reported on its front page. "And now the last trench has been carried by Amazonian assault, and the whole citadel of learning lies open and defenceless...."

Philippa Fawcett worked as a scholar all her life. In May 1948, the Royal Family of the UK passed a decree that women could from now on graduate from Cambridge. Philippa, who was then 80 years old, was delighted. She died a month later.

THE PENNILESS YOUTH WHO AMAZED THE PROFESSORS

WHAT WOULD HAPPEN IF you took the brain of one of the greatest geniuses who ever lived, and put it in the head of a penniless, starving boy in one of the poorest parts of Asia?

Well, it seems that God or Destiny or Fate once did exactly that.

Teenager Srinivasa Ramanujan was so poor that he could not afford the cheapest food in the cheapest shop.

The year was 1906, and he lived in India, in the area known as Madras. At 18 years old, he was starving so badly that he almost died.

He had to beg his friends to give him something to eat and a place to sleep. And then he went knocking on doors in Madras city to see if he could find a job as a lowly clerk in an office. He had no qualifications or work experience to offer.

The only thing he knew for sure was that he was good at maths — he had won several mathematics prizes when he had been a child at school, in happier times.

He managed to stay alive into his early 20s, and tried to get a job at the tax office. There he met a tax man who loved numbers and had started the Indian Mathematical Society.

"I can do maths," said Ramanujan. "Look at my notebooks."

The tax officer looked at the notebooks and realized that the young man was not just good at maths, but astonishingly brilliant. The number puzzles the young man was experimenting with were the sort of thing that top mathematicians played with.

If an uneducated person, who until recently had been little more than a beggar, could do this in his head without training, he must have an astonishing brain.

Instead of giving him a job in the tax office, the man recommended that Ramanujan write articles about mathematics for research journals.

But the young man also had to earn money to live, so Ramamujan did that in his spare time while he struggled with lowly jobs. This carried on for years, until another helpful man decided to send the young man's extraordinary equations to what he felt was the cleverest place on earth — Cambridge University in the UK.

The first two Cambridge professors who received them showed no interest. They probably were too busy or too lazy to read them. But the third one took the time to really examine them and realized that what he was looking at was really mind-blowing.

This professor, whose name was G.H. Hardy, invited the young Indian boy to board a ship to the UK.

After much opposition from his penniless parents (and reluctance on his own part), he eventually travelled across the world and settled in the UK.

In Cambridge, it became obvious that Ramanujan was a rare genius. He wrote thousands of mathematical formulas. These were so amazing that other mathematicians studied them for years.

He was invited to join the Royal Society, which was a club for the world's top scientists.

But because of his poor background and the malnutrition he had suffered, he was never healthy. He died in 1920, aged just 32 years old.

Recently, the Indian government declared that his birthday, December 22, would be declared National Mathematics Day.

Today, all over the planet, people celebrate the genius of the poor boy with the amazing brain, and lament the fact that had the world been kinder to him, he might have achieved much more.

THE GOOD WITCH WHO MADE AN AMAZING DECISION

MARIA HAD A GREAT RELATIONSHIP with her father.

But then her parents had another child. And another. And another. And another. And another. And another. And so on — until the girl was eventually the eldest of 21 children!

How did Maria manage to keep his attention?

It was very, very hard — but she did it by being very, very brilliant. By the time she was 13 years old, she could speak Italian, French, Latin, Greek, German, Spanish and Hebrew.

And it wasn't just languages she was good at: she became a master of philosophy and mathematics. In those days, the 1700s, those were the top subjects at universities.

Her father, a professor, often invited other professors to their house in Italy to show off his clever oldest daughter.

But deep down, there was something wrong. Maria Agnesi's father liked to show off how super-smart his child was. But in her heart she did not value that type of knowledge. She was a quiet, introverted girl who thought being kind and good-hearted was much more important than being clever.

Still, it seemed that circumstances had made it important that she be seen as clever, so she did smart things.

One of her great discoveries was a mathematics formula which produced numbers to draw on graph paper, making a special type of curved (or turning) line. No one had ever made that formula before.

It was called the "aversiera" which means "a turn" in Italian. But "aversiera" is also a short form for the similar word "avversiere", which means "wife of the devil" or "witch". So thanks to a translation mistake, her famous algebraic equation went down in history under the English name "the witch of Agnesi".

This was odd, because Maria Agnesi was the opposite of what we might think of as a witch. She was gentle and spiritual.

In 1750, Pope Benedict XIV appointed this brilliant young woman professor of science and mathematics at a university — which was extraordinary, since women in those days were not even allowed to be students, let alone professors.

But to everyone's amazement, Maria turned down the job, and after her father died in 1752, she stopped doing mathematics and science completely.

This hyper-intelligent woman said that all her genius had taught her one extraordinary thing: that being good was more important than being clever.

She became a nun and spent the rest of her life looking after the poor and the sick. She was buried with the inmates of a home for penniless women when she died at the age of 81.

Some people thought it was a pity that such a clever woman had decided to drop her studies in science and mathematics.

But many people, when they thought about it, realized that with the choices she made, Maria had taught the whole world the most important lesson of all: perhaps life really is not about being rich and successful, but about being the person you were meant to be.

KEEP READING

READING ABOUT THE LIVES of scientists and other discoverers adds to our store of knowledge, but we hope also leads us towards something much greater, which is wisdom.

This book is part of a series, which we hope you'll enjoy reading, and will spur you on to do your own scientific research.

The creators of this book wish you success in your explorations.

THE YOUNG SCIENTISTS SERIES

Book 1: SECRETS IN THE ROCKS
Five Astounding Tales of People Solving Mysteries Beneath Our Feet

Book 2: FABULOUS PHYSICS
Five Amazing Stories of People Who Solved Nature's Puzzles

Book 3: MAGICAL MATHEMATICS
Five Astonishing Stories of People Who Did Miracles with Numbers

Book 4: BREAKERS OF BARRIERS
Five Stunning Stories of People Demolishing Walls to Make History

Book 5: SCIENTIFIC PIONEERS
Five Incredible Tales of People Who Helped Develop the Scientific Method

Book 6: THE AMAZING QUANTUM
Five Awesome Stories of People Who Made a Revolution in Physics

Book 7: THE SCIENCE OF HUMANITY
Five Fascinating Stories of People Who Helped Us Understand Ourselves

Book 8: WOMEN OF DISCOVERY
Five Super Stories of Fabulous Females Who Made Scientific History

Book 9: THE INVENTOR'S SPARK
Five Marvelous Stories of People Who Helped Shape the Modern World

Book 10: ADVANCES IN ALCHEMY
Five Startling Stories of Chemistry and Biology

Book 11: THE CALL OF THE STARS
Five Wonderful Stories of People Looking to the Heavens

Book 12: MYSTERIES OF NATURE'S LAWS
Five Striking Stories of People Investigating the Deepest Puzzles of Reality

Published by

WS Education, an imprint of
World Scientific Publishing Co. Pte. Ltd.
5 Toh Tuck Link, Singapore 596224
USA office: 27 Warren Street, Suite 401-402, Hackensack, NJ 07601
UK office: 57 Shelton Street, Covent Garden, London WC2H 9HE

National Library Board, Singapore Cataloguing in Publication Data
Name(s): Vittachi, Nury, 1958– | Cheung, Step, illustrator.
Title: Magical mathematics : five astonishing stories of people who did miracles with numbers / author, Nury Vittachi ; illustrator, Step Cheung.
Other title(s): Young scientists series ; 3.
Description: Singapore : World Scientific Publishing Co Pte Ltd, 2017.
Identifier(s): OCN 969702860 | ISBN 978-981-3221-40-6 (paperback)
Subject(s): LCSH: Mathematicians--Juvenile literature. | Scientists--Juvenile literature. | Mathematics--Juvenile literature. | Science--Juvenile literature.
Classification: DDC 510.922--dc23

British Library Cataloguing-in-Publication Data
A catalogue record for this book is available from the British Library.

All royalties received will be channelled to the National Book Development Council of Singapore (NBDCS) as a gift from the author.

First published 2017
Reprinted 2018

Printed in Singapore